Strange Currencies

STRANGE CURRENCIES

A Collection of Poems by

Daniel Sendecki

Introduction by Jesse Glass

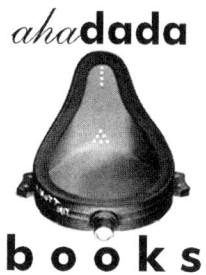

Copyright © Daniel Sendecki 2003
Introduction copyright © Jesse Glass 2003

All rights reserved. The use of any part of this publication transmitted in any form or by any means, electronic, mechanical, photocopying, recording, or otherwise, or stored in a retrieval system, without the prior consent of the publisher, is an infringement of the copyright law.

First Edition
Printed and bound in Canada

Visit Ahadada Books web site:
www.ahadadabooks.com

National Library of Canada Cataloguing in Publication

Sendecki, Daniel, 1975-
Strange currencies / Daniel Sendecki.

ISBN 0-9732233-0-8
I. Title.

PS8587.E543S77 2003   C811'.6   C2002-9061369
       PR9199.3.S395S77 2003

Contents

Introduction vii

The East Window 13
I Enter the World as a Tourist 17
The Physics of Flocking 19
Out of Hanoi Endlessly Spinning 21
Lipstick 23
Six Exposures 25
Sometimes Classrooms Become 27
Prisoner 166 29
Hushed Conversations 31
American Bombshell 33
A Child Runs After His Brother 35
Ramayana 37
Night Train to Bangkok 39
Koh Samui 41
The Shine of Stars 43
The Promise of Sleep 45
Calcutta 47
Walt Whitman Descends Upon India 49
California Oranges 51
I Saw the Dead of America 53
The Passengers 55
Strange Currencies 57
Collapse of Suns 59
Facing West 61
Consecration 63

Chronology 64

Introduction

    Young poets always seem to be taking trips until they get older. They seem to need to move themselves across space & time in order to meet the Shadow that rises before or beneath or behind them. As in Arthur Gordon Pym's ending with the circling Tekeli-li! Birds & the huge white featureless Shadow rising to embrace him, young poets are just like that impossible Pym, with the sound of the cataracts and the canoe speeding steadily forward into the unknown. We know Pym survives, because he returns to tell us his story in his piping birth-cry of a voice, and we guess that the journey he takes is a mental odyssey tricked out in the gingerbread of 19th century American high literature. Borges, on his own keen-sighted foray, suspected as much.

    Going to worlds outside of Europe & N. America is a kind of elaborate self-inhumation for Western people, and young poets in particular. The Other threatens to swallow them up. This swallowing can sometimes be pleasant in prospect as in Rimbaud's dreams of scientific research and amassing fortunes; however, the process itself can often become an agonizing one as in Rimbaud's trip in a palanquin across miles of desert with a cancerous leg. Ultimately, for manylike Pym, Rimbaud and the writer of this volumethe Other disgorges the traveler after many travails and he returns to his native land with stories ready to recount that amaze, teach, uplift, warn, or console. On the other hand, those young poets that choose to grow old in the presence of the Other & far away from their native language can be likened to the three

Innocents sealed by Nebuchadnezzar inside the fiery furnace. Often their songs are barely heeded, & are mistaken for echoes, sighs, & groans by the Listeners they left behind. The Angel that marches with them up & down among the flames saves their lives, but rarely saves their words.

  Lucky the poet, then, who returns from his journey while still young, with his visions (and his language!) still intact! Daniel Sendecki is just such a poet. We need not examine his itinerary, for it is given in detail elsewhere. Instead, a few words about Sendecki's sincerity are in order, for this is what sets *Strange Currencies* apart from typical tourist poetry. Sendecki's eyes are not those of a jaded traveler of 2002 A.D. Instead, it is from his great sincerity that he sees, and it is this same gift that allows him to bridge the gap between Self and Other, if only in flashes and if only for one luminous poem in this volume. Please don't misunderstand me: there are many fine poems & memorable tropes between these covers. When Daniel Sendecki tells us that Calcutta is "...something like watching a human organ at work with the skin pulled back under a theatre of lights...." we believe him. Moreover, we can only marvel when, in "Facing West" he delivers a hymn to his future home-coming in which he sees a "cat's cradle of water droplets" connecting continents, & goes on to deliver lines the skillful music of which place him firmly as an equal among contemporary English language poets. But there is one poem that is worth the price of this book. In it we find Daniel Sendecki at his most sincere, and I believe it heralds great things for the future of this young poet. "A Child Runs After His Brother" is the record of one moment in which the Other is no longer history, novelty, or potent Shadow, but assumes the Human Form Divine written of by William Blake, and it can be found on page 35. Reader, see for yourself. Then follow Daniel Sendecki's voyage across Asia and into his own maturity as a poet. In the end he will not disappoint you. In his "Consecration" he gives us these lines as a parting gift:

> May you laugh, may you laugh,
> Like hail falling on a tin roof, may you laugh.

With the roar of silence in your heart,
To lose again what you've found out,
May you laugh.

    I say Amen to this new Singer who offers us both sincerity & hilarity. Welcome & Amen.

Jesse Glass
Shin-Urayasu, Japan
1/11/2003.
The Year of the Sheep.

In beauty I walk
With beauty before me I walk
With beauty behind me I walk
With beauty above me I walk
With beauty above & about me I walk
It is finished in beauty
It is finished in beauty

- Translation from the Navajo
  by Washington Matthews[1]

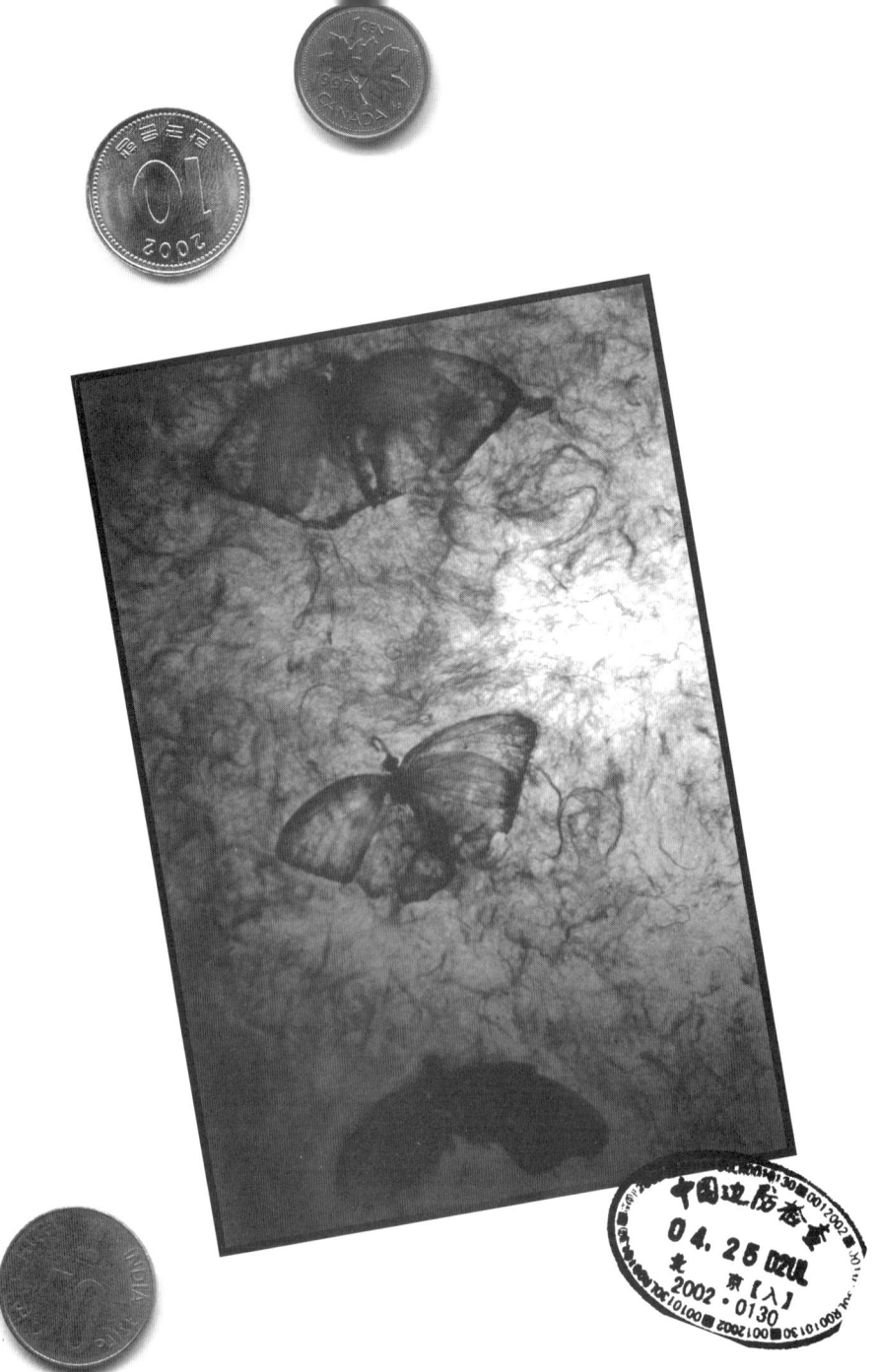

THE EAST WINDOW

When I close my eyes
against the eastern sun I don't
see the backs of my eyelids:
black, blank pages
faintly glowing in the
dissipating sunrise.

What I see is
a palimpsest
of confessions.

(though I presume the blank page's
somewhere
what's left of it
anyway)

It was never a page
unblemished,
offering freedom,
never exactly
untouched & pristine,
but it was enough.

A place to begin.

We set sail at dawn. The red sun,
a paper lantern, set fire
to the open sky of Chu.

Turning east, the sun between stacks
swung in the dawn.
The big machines of government
pulled back the hems of mountains
revealing flesh and clay.
Birds wheeled in the morning,
under a ceiling of broken clouds,
through sunlight strung at
curious angles,
wings
shining
like the faces of
Chinese tourists
opening fanwise from below deck.
Emerging from the shadows,
into the bright Yangzi morning
to witness the boundless falling away[2]
of a million people.

Loneliness chooses its language
in the syncopation
of feet
winding up through the gorge,
the familiar track
linking futures over the vanished ridge.
Walls of stone, upstream to the west
will come, presently, tomorrow,
to hold back Wushan's clouds and rain
until a smooth lake rises in the narrow gorges.[3]

We stay above deck
until the heavy sky lies over the river,
growing black in the late light and
arc lights lick out empty windows
of vacant skyscrapers.

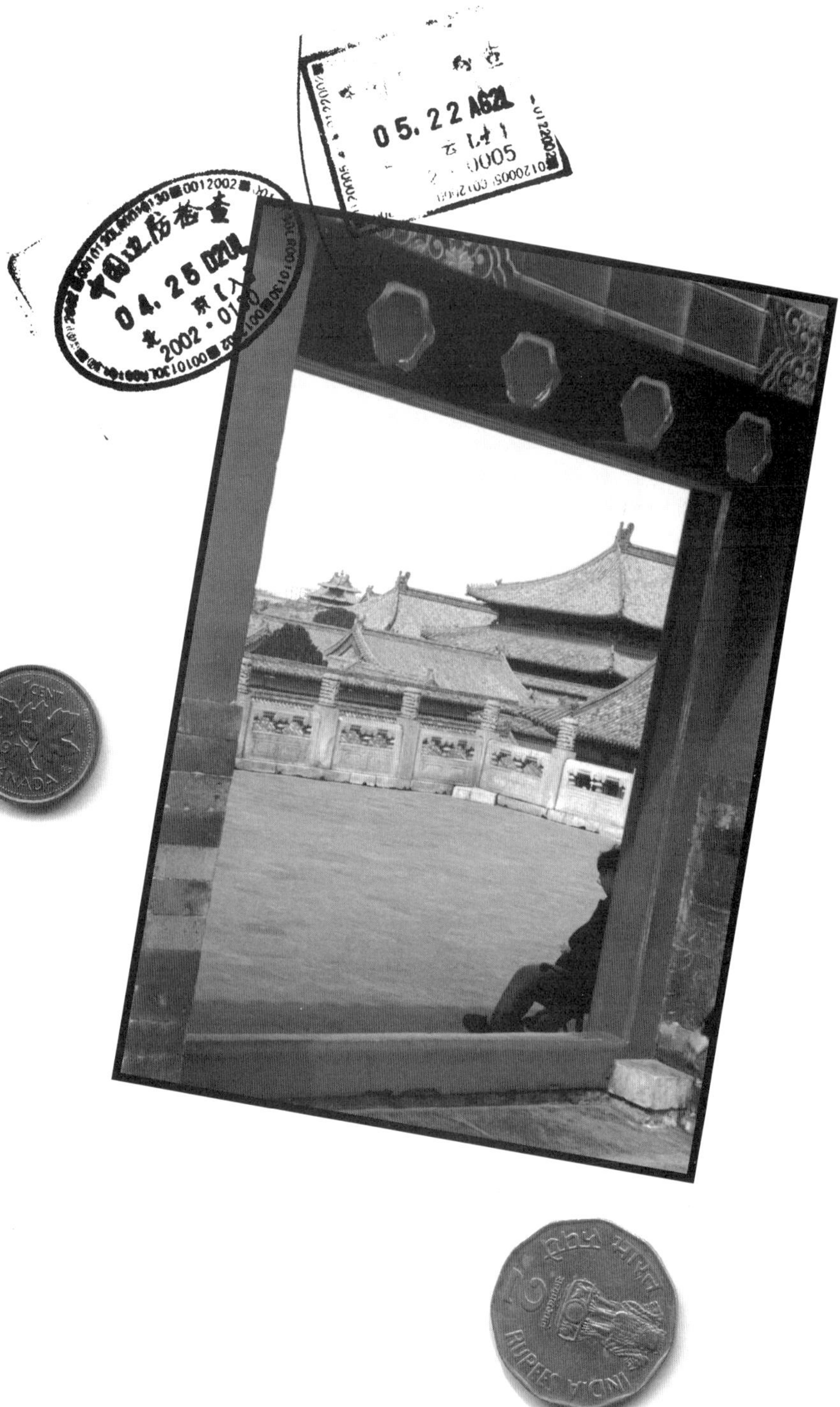
05.22
中国边防检查
04.25
2002
CANADA
CENT
INDIA
RUPEES

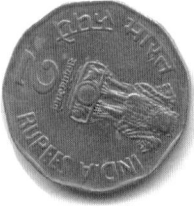

I Enter the World as a Tourist

As I sit in Tian'anmen Square
eating a Big Mac and drinking a Coke
over the nucleus of a country's rupture
I enter the world as a tourist;
am become invisible
like the dead son of an Inuit tribe
that welcomes its children
into the source of meaning
by naming them through their environment.
Snow, Sun, River — names in which are conjoined
and condensed a person whose past and con-
tinuity coincide with the word
until the child dies or is married
off and the word is never to be
repeated or refound.

What word did you stop repeating when you
learned of my absence?

The Physics of Flocking

Most nights I drift right off to sleep. But sometimes I lie here, hugging the pillow, watching the pattern the headlights make on the wall, listening to Saigon outside my window: cyclos and motorbikes darting through the streets, like swarms of two-stroke bumblebees spitting exhaust. Moving *en masse*, as if they possess – like insects or birds in flight – the intuitive ability to sense in which direction the group will hasten. And like this they continue, and occasionally one or two will fall off to drone down back alleys or splash through puddles and disappear.

Nights like those, I want to curl myself around silence, tighten around its surface. Make myself as small as possible.

OUT OF HANOI ENDLESSLY SPINNING

      I,
        sitting at the vortex of this carousel,
out of Buddhist altars and herb sellers
        blurred into hemivision,
out of old men begging for
        dollars, their faces as pinched up
        and scarred as a tractor tire lashed
        to a pier,
out of tin box makers and gravestones
        giggling past my doorway,
weave butterfly nets of words
        to chase down the barefoot beauty
        of the women curling through traffic.
The memory of their faces.

LIPSTICK

On the steps of Saigon's Notre Dame Cathedral,
where ceaseless traffic flows,
preternaturally – a murder of a million crows –
I withdraw into the shadow of a high-rise.

Out in the sun, the poor spear tourists with their eyes.
Each tries, in vain, to neither notice nor react.
Next to me, out of my reach,
a woman fixes her makeup in a cracked compact:
her lipstick dries the colour of fear.

Six Exposures

1/
Phnom Penh is a spill of whitewashed buildings heaped together on the shore of the Mekong like bones bleaching in the sun.

2/
Under the high eaves of the Foreign Correspondents Club sunburnt tourists divine their futures in the runes of ice-cubes settling in sweating glasses.

3/
Suspended in the ground, fleshless skulls shine inviolate like stars arranged in fallen constellations.

4/
Roadside children collect lotus flowers to weave into bracelets while, feet away, latent and unseen, landmines lie underground like knives asleep in kitchen drawers imagining meat.

5/
Roots of Banyan trees slowly and incessantly cleave apart the carved-sandstone knees of celestial nymphs.

6/
In Siem Reap a girl gets married,
and she is so afraid and sad that she gets
up on the back of a water buffalo and cries.

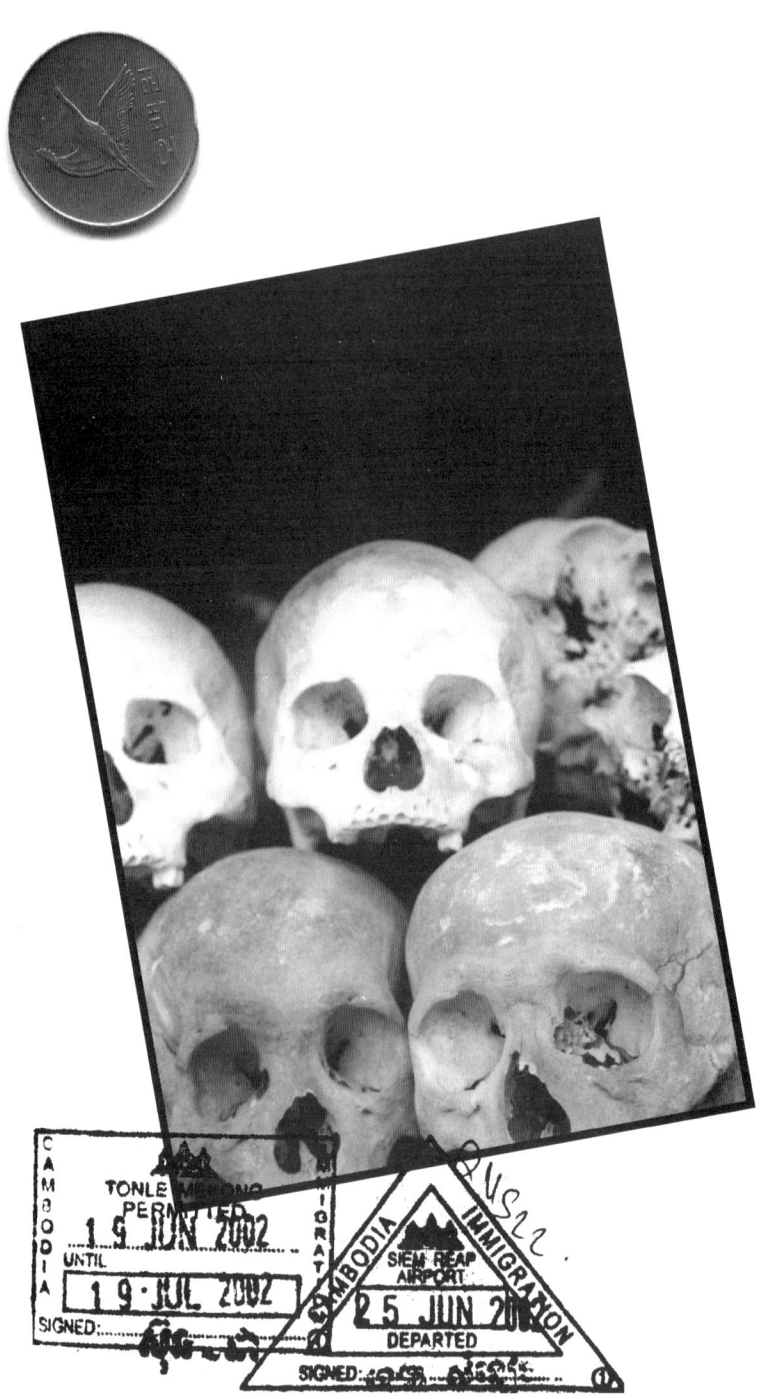

Sometimes Classrooms Become

In 1975, Tuol Svay Prey High School was taken over by Pol Pot's security forces and turned into a prison known as Security Prison 21; over 17,000 people were interned here and eventually put to death.

Sometimes classrooms become especially beautiful when all the students have been dismissed, and chalk dust turns slowly in shafts of dusklight. So in a poem about darkness one sees a little freedom, a little light. Standing inside, around us, the numbered photos of prisoners hang from all four walls. Their eyes, behind a grime of dots, form star-maps of fear, confusion, and despair. And in each photo the prisoners carry with them their deaths, like tents, to be pitched in the killing fields.

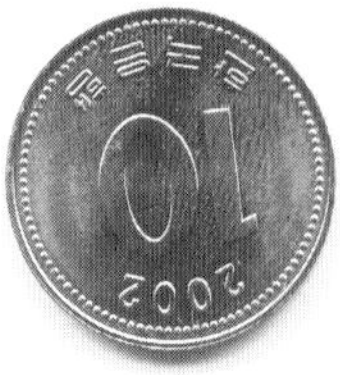

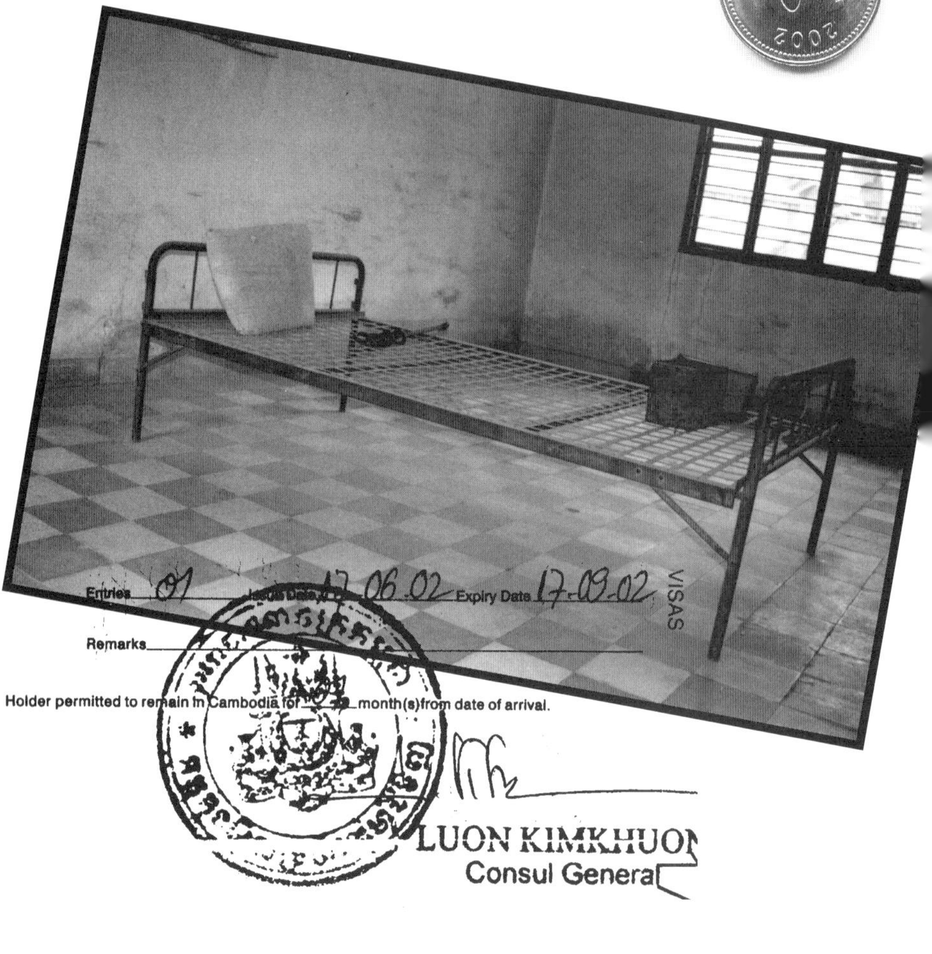

Entries 01 Issue Date 17.06.02 Expiry Date 17-09-02 VISAS

Remarks

Holder permitted to remain in Cambodia for [illegible] month(s) from date of arrival.

LUON KIMKHUON
Consul General

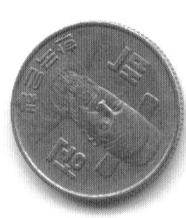

Prisoner 166

    I. PERFORATING GUNSHOT WOUND TO ANTERIOR — WITH:

        A. PERFORATIONS OF STERNUM, AORTA, LUNG, THIRD THORACIC VERTEBRA, SPINAL CORD.

        B. MARKED MEDIASTINAL HEMORRHAGE.

        C. HEMOTHORACES.

CAUSE OF DEATH: GUNSHOT WOUND TO TRUNK WITH PERFORATION OF AORTA, SPINAL CORD, AND LUNGS.

He might as well have been asleep,
prone on the bare cot,
a smile fastened tightly
over his mouth,
reading the backs of his eyelids
like a book of answers
no man has ever written.

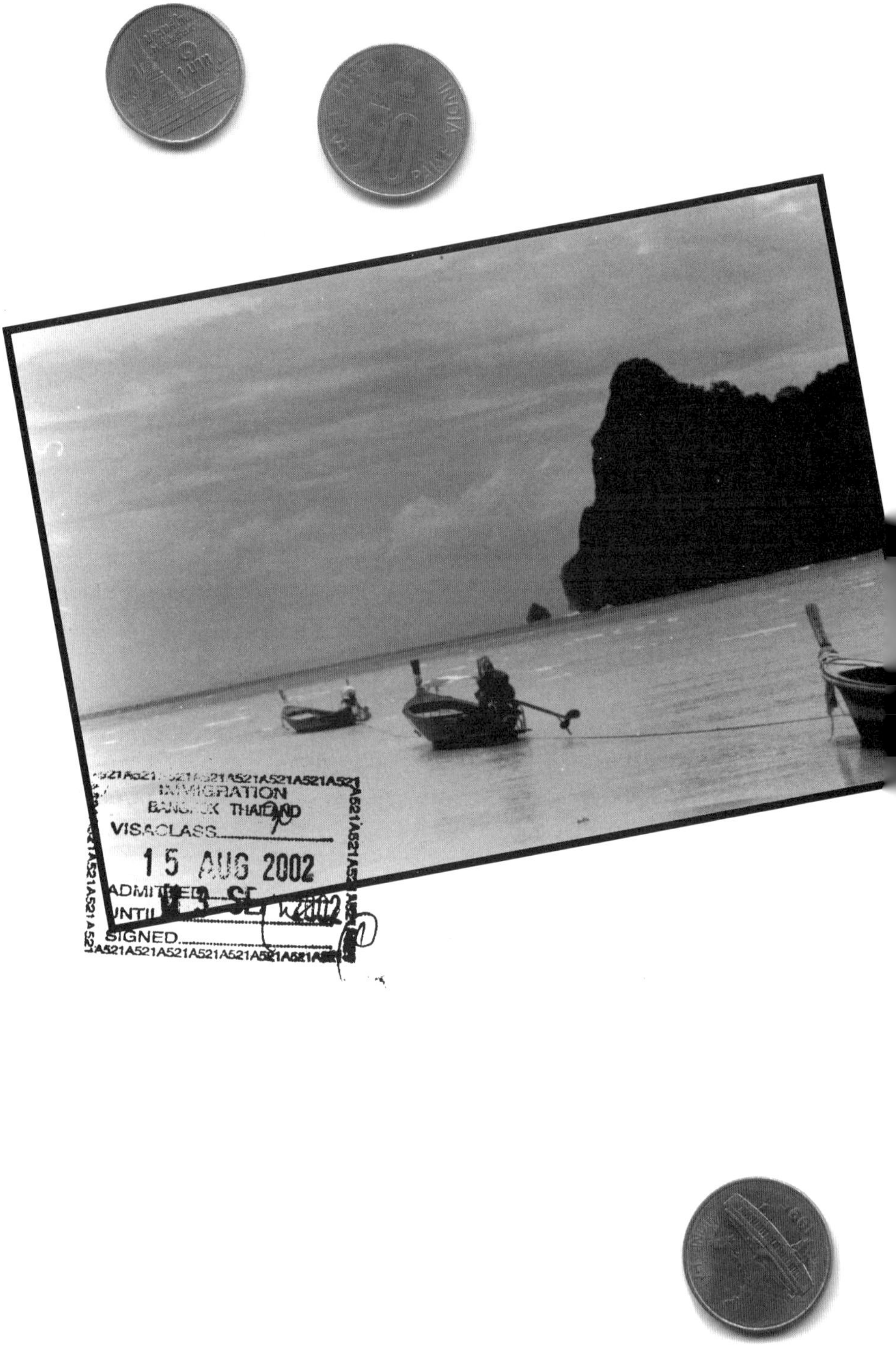
IMMIGRATION
VISA CLASS
15 AUG 2002
ADMITTED
UNTIL
SIGNED

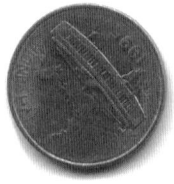

Hushed Conversations

Palm trees stood huddled in groups leaning out over the Mekong River, engaged in hushed conversations like thin surgeons trying to diagnose a cancer; the tourist speedboats plied the river in an orgy of sound and speed — their outboard motors thrashed the water like parasites churning in blood.

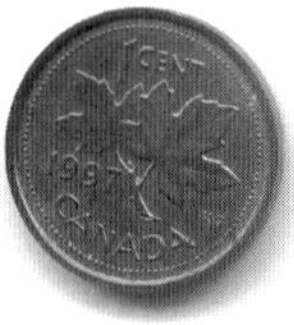
1 CENT
1997
CANADA

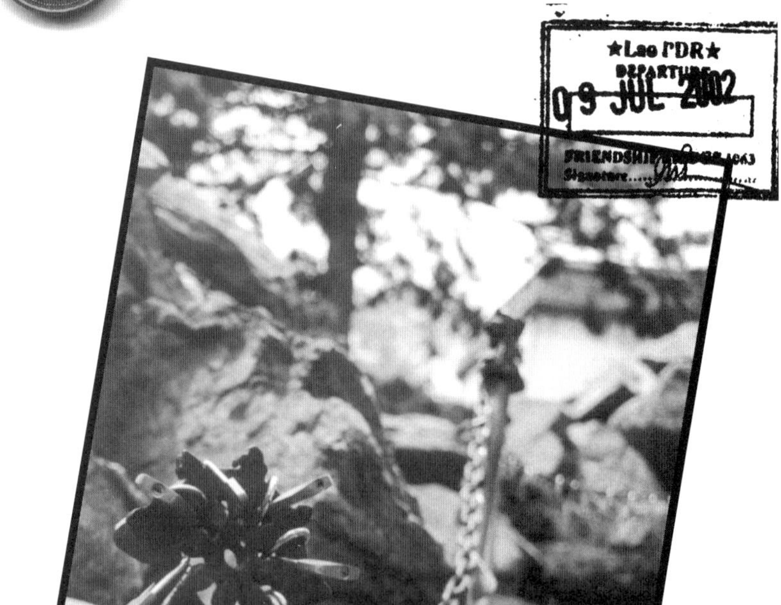
★Lao PDR★
DEPARTURE
09 JUL 2002

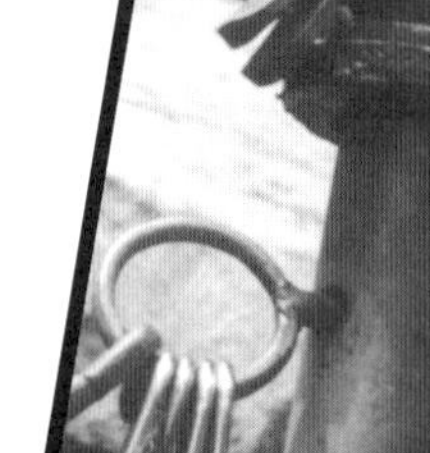

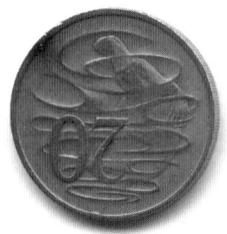

AMERICAN BOMBSHELL

And there are always, everywhere, hidden behind stilt houses and juxtaposed against Buddhist temples, the reminders of conflict, being eaten by time and water, being converted to the strangest uses: an old American bombshell, once carrying a payload of gunpowder and shrapnel, turned nose down in a flower garden and holding up a lotus blossom; an impotent Russian-built anti-aircraft gun frustrated into a makeshift merry-go-round by giggling Lao schoolchildren.

A Child Runs After His Brother

It's here, in Laos, that one experiences inexplicable beauty: a child runs after his brother through the streets — the white soles of his bare feet appearing like new stars against the inky dusk — and his laughing brother shouting encouragement in a beautiful language I could never pretend to understand.

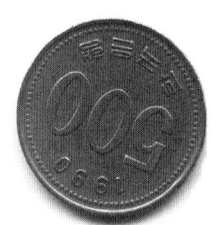

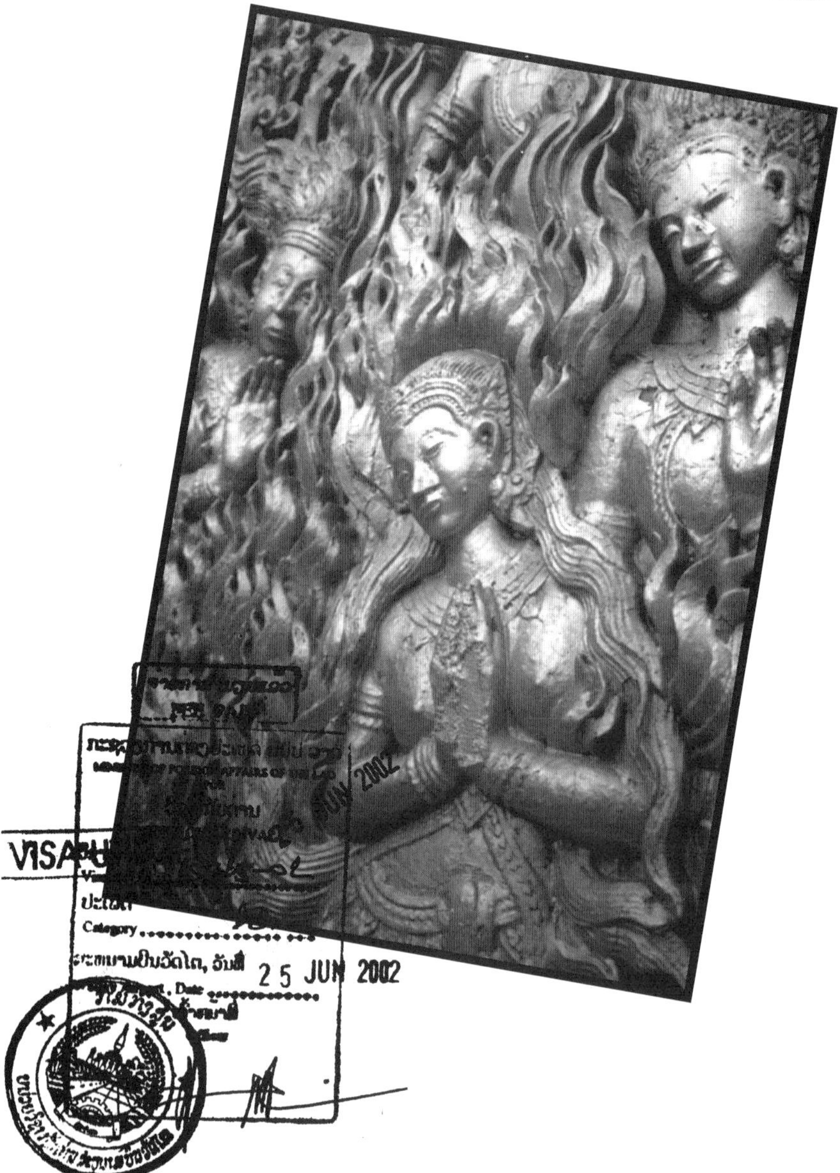
VISA
Category
25 JUN 2002

Ramayana

Beautiful and remote, the Royal Dancers moved sedately across the floor of the Palace Hall. Behind them, the walls were covered in shards of colourful glass — arranged in scenes of village life and Lao legend. The dancers were re-enacting the "Ramayana": their feet moving in short, thoughtful steps; their arches curling and lifting them; their perfect postures and steady unmoving chins; their arms like the necks of swan, rolling and dipping; their gracefully arranged fingers — their bodies entire moved in measured, fluid, concert. As the sun curved below the mountains, the room shone scarlet and rose and had the dancers not persisted in their careful movements, I would have thought them subjects on a wet canvas, their forms outlined in thick dollops of colour and the whole room churned by an artist's brush.

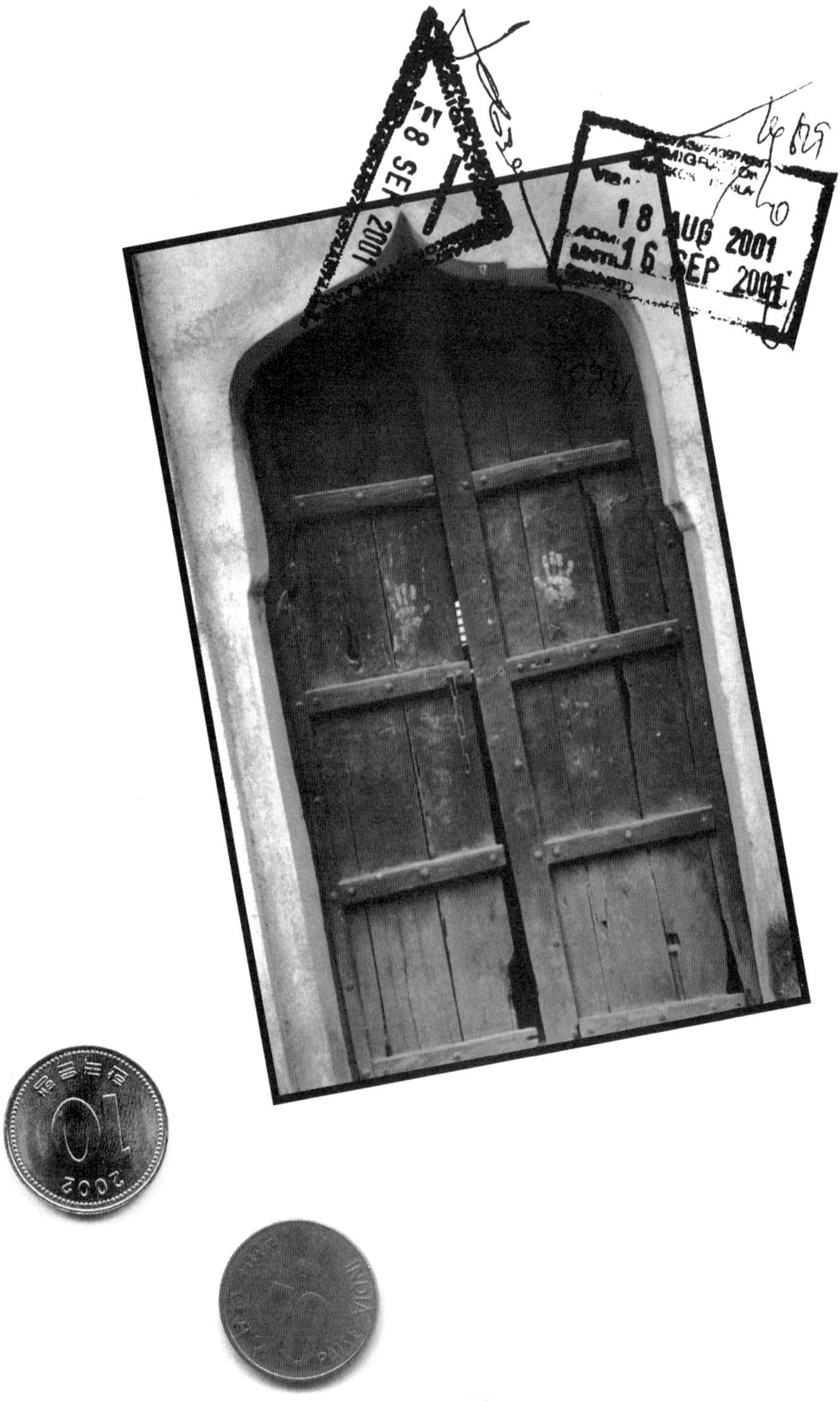
18 AUG 2001
16 SEP 2001
2002
INDIA

Night Train to Bangkok

The atmosphere of the border — there is something about it like a baptism. First, the exhilaration of passing through no-man's-land absolved of citizenship; neither resident nor tourist of any country. Then, your eyes beginning to open at Passport Control like those of a newborn child awakened during the sacrament. Awakened, of course, not to the possibilities of new beginnings but to a glass half empty; a passport anointed with the ink of the entry permit. Finally, the immigration officer handing you back your unfinished life and everything that is beautiful and ugly about your person.

So it was like this I crossed the border into Thailand at Nong Khai and took the night train to Bangkok.

15 AUG 2002

40

Koh Samui

Need and despair,
       of course,
are only agents
promoting the efficient
transmission of loneliness.
       Thus,
this is less a poem than
an open sore
       enlisted to induce
       the memory
       on a cellular level
       of Koh Samui,
11 September 2001.
       A single gecko on
       a white wall.
       A tangle of sheets at
       the foot of a hotel room
       bed.
       A bullet hole
       framing the landscape
       of my soul:
the knowledge that everyone I touch
will come to feel this way,
       eventually.

42

THE SHINE OF STARS

At night, breezes pass with perfect ease about the whole earth to touch me wherever I sleep: the night air of Halong Bay, charged with the shine of stars; the yawn of Hanoi; the fitful cough of Saigon; the heavy panting of Phnom Penh rolling with the scent of the Mekong; the breezes issuing from the mountains of northern Laos, pregnant with the vapours of clouds; sweet with the stink of rot and life, the heaving sigh of Bangkok — all come to my side at night, whispering: "Truly a kind of heaven, this."

44

THE PROMISE OF SLEEP

Walt Whitman and I
are impelled by an anxious desire
that draws us about the world:
the vague notion that we're
one hotel room away from the centre,
from the confluence of birth and decay,
from the promise of sleep in the beautiful
uncut silence of night,
a silence that presupposes silence
under a crown of stars.

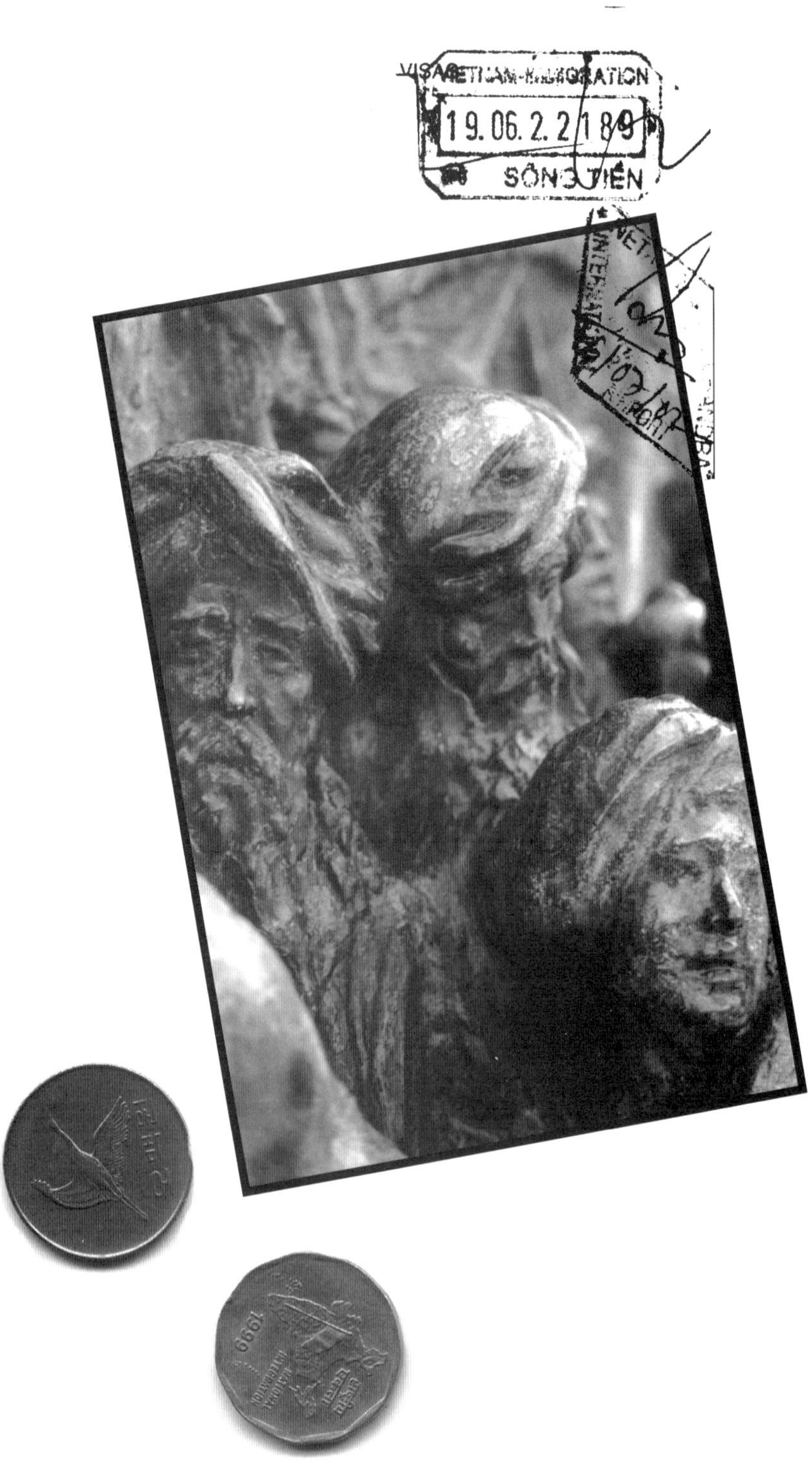
SÔNG TIỀN

CALCUTTA

In the day Calcutta is more flesh than city. Knotted and beating, all that is not flesh — iron, glass, and concrete — rises up from the ground and leans into the smoke and exhaust. The Ganges – here it is called the Hooghly – is wound inextricably through Calcutta like a pulmonary artery choked with plaque. Everywhere people and animals are spilled across roadways – like spears of rice to be threshed under the weight of the traffic – waiting through the dry months for the rains with upturned eyes. Just as when you observe the pictures so exactly described in *Gray's Anatomy* you have the sensation in Calcutta of a profound mystery. It is, I thought, resting for a moment on a bridge that spans the holiest of rivers, something like watching a human organ at work with the skin pulled back under a theatre of lights. There isn't a town of any size which does not contain some of the agony and beauty of Calcutta.

VISAS

REPUBLIC of KOREA
대한민국
IMMIGRATION
2001. AUG. 18
DEPARTED
INCHEON AIRPORT 078

REPUBLIC of KOREA
대한민국
IMMIGRATION
ADMITTED
2001. SEP. 08
UNTIL

INCHEON AIRPORT 148

WALT WHITMAN DESCENDS UPON INDIA[4]

in a spotless airplane and lands in a
city where tourists sleep in white-tiled rooms
and dream room-service dreams of a Calcutta
that is no longer cruel, not a city
even but a stage whereupon he can
abstract himself from the cast and
reassure himself that this is not death,
nor that hunger, surely not wounds, those
but a festival elaborately
choreographed for the benefit
of his amusement
and sanitized for his protection.

With pens stolen from hotel lobbies
in the margins of a Gideon's bible.
my poems grow in slow gestation.

I tried once to set them free
but in the absence of their surrogate
mother they lost all meaning.

I dreamed that Walt Whitman and I
buried books of poems, until,
suspended in the ground
their fleshless spines shone inviolate
like stars arranged in fallen constellations;
until the whole world seemed to
glow in our crime.

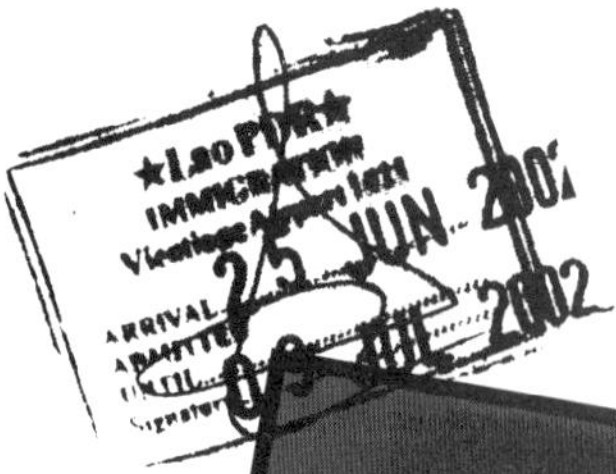
25 JUN 2002
ARRIVAL

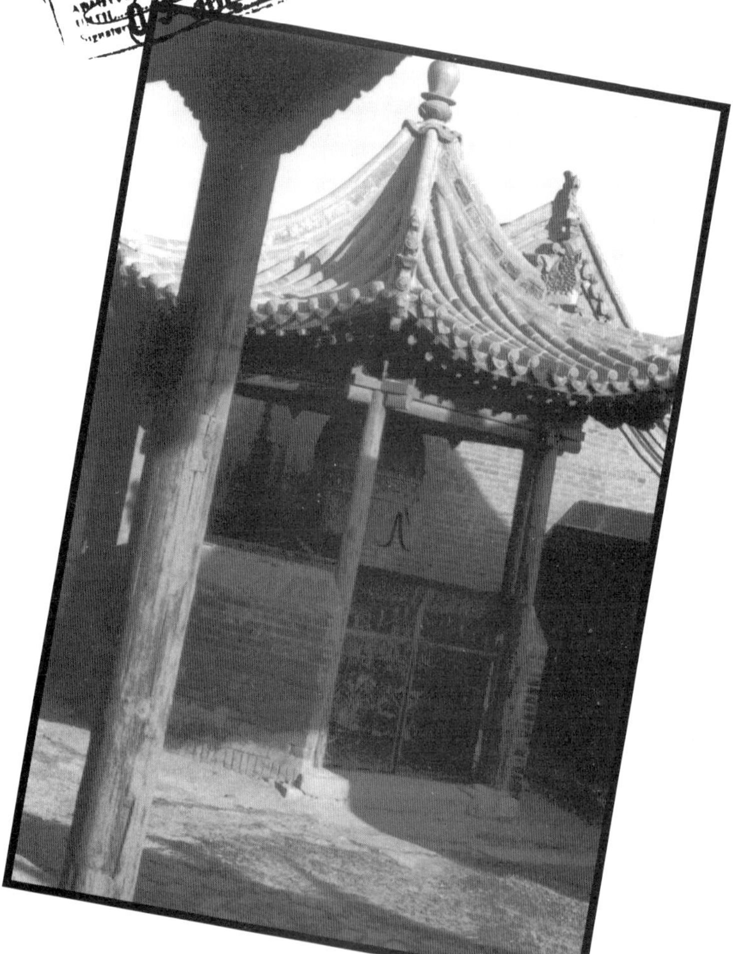

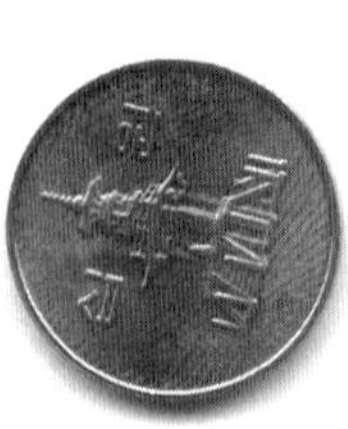

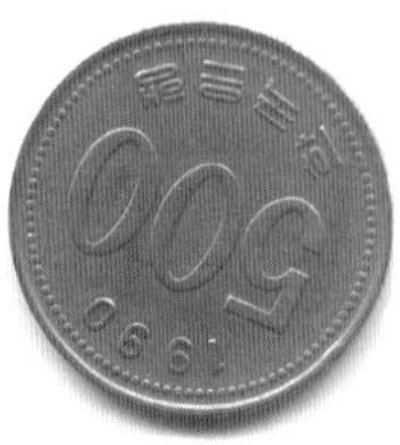

California Oranges

My Walt Whitman
is an American accountant
from Berkeley
whose awkward silences
follow him, doggedly
stopping at every
corner of his conversation
to sell California oranges and
star maps of his defeats.
He sounds his barbaric yawp
over the roofs of the world
on a cell phone.

52

I Saw the Dead of America

On the shores of the Ganges
I saw the dead of America
raised in pink chalk by a young boy.
He drew a pink airplane next
to two pink towers.
    "Who's that?" I asked, pointing
at the pilot.
    "Osama Bin Laden." (He
outlined windows with the help
of a milk carton)
    "He's got a beard," I said.

In the windows he drew pink flames.

My latest poem
is inscribed in a hotel
basin in an alphabet
of whiskers
haunted by drains.

54

The Passengers

On the platform lanterns gather back the night with thin fingers of light and young girls pass with slow step among the benches selling cigarettes and old coins. The passengers are at a loss impatiently smoking and swatting at flies. The night train to Varanasi is overdue and we are all hungry for a little more geography in which to consider our own dissatisfaction.

56

Strange Currencies

This wind offers no
relief an
asthmatic breeze
in truth and we're
road thin and
wheezing through
Delhi's dusk.
Women make nets to thread
across alleys
we'll walk through
not knowing
until it's too late &
we wake in hotel
rooms
fumbling with our
belt buckles
like strange
currencies.

58

COLLAPSE OF SUNS

Hunger is that dizzying space between sunrise and sunset
when her body, gutted by poverty, slides through Delhi's
    traffic
in a repeated rehearsal of disappointment until her eyes,
like collapsed suns, lull me into their orbit,
and I imagine some beauty in the event
while forgetting my breakfast of ham and eggs, coffee,
    cigarette.

JAPAN IMMIGRATION
上 陸 許 可
22 DEC. 2001
在留資格 短 期 滞 在
Status: Temporary Visitor
90 days
IMMIGRATION
出 国
DEPARTED
入国審査官-日本国
NARITA(2)
28. DEC. 2001
IMMIGRATION
1268
INDIA
1980

FACING WEST

In Tokyo's veiny dusk, vapour trails
become rope in the fingers of my mind,
crisscross the darkening sky; a cat's cradle
of water droplets connects continents
thousands of miles distant and hums with
vibrations of home so vivid had I
arms strong and delicate enough I would
draw them down, hand over hand, until mist
lay in bales all around and I saw,
corporeal and magnificent, the
lights of Vancouver and farther on, the
luminescent caps of mountains bent
in the slow marriage of continents.
You've never been so much mine;
never so close, never so far away.

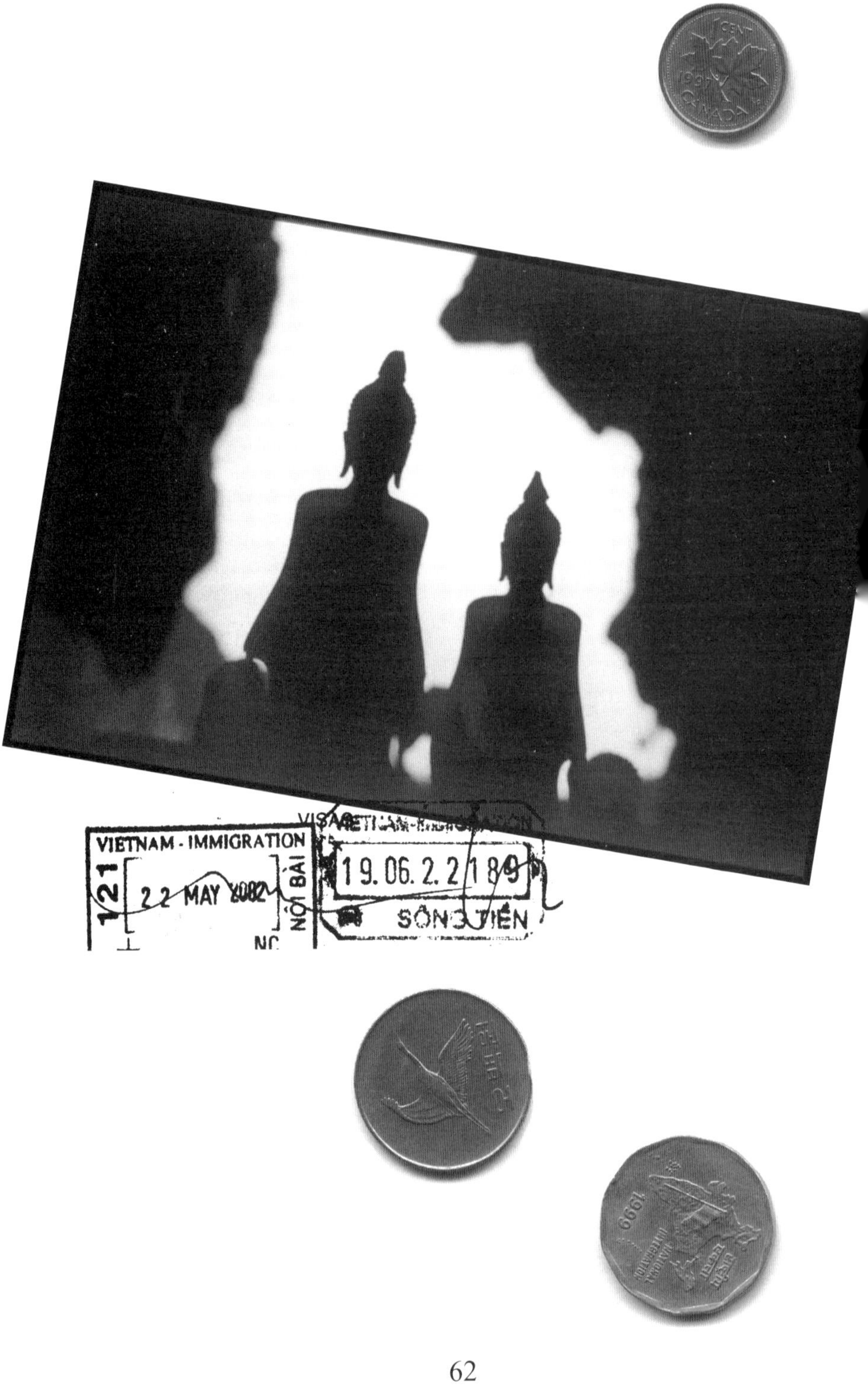

CONSECRATION[5]

May your heart become a thin vein of copper.
May you become an antenna crying though the night
for sounds thin spun by space and time.
May yours be a melody of absence:
the sucking and sobbing of flowers,
the dance of water seeping upwards.

May you laugh, may you laugh,
Like hail falling on a tin roof, may you laugh.
With the roar of silence in your heart,
To lose again what you've found out,
May you laugh.

CHRONOLOGY

April 25	Arrives in Beijing; travels through Shanxi Province and the Inner Mongolian Highland. Visits the Forbidden City, Xuan Kong Xi, and the Yungang Caves.
May 11	Leaves northern China and moves westward toward the Guanzhong Plain in Shaanxi province. Visits the Qin Terracotta Warriors.
May 12	Arrives in Xi'an and continues westward into the Sichuan Province. Visits Qingcheng Mountain, the birthplace of Taoism.
May 16	Arrives in Chengdu and moves eastward up the Yiangze towards Yichang. Returns to Xi'an.
May 23	Flies from Xi'an to Guangzhou and continues onward to Hanoi.
May 24	Arrives in Hanoi, Vietnam. Detained briefly.
May 29	Sets out north of Hanoi to visit Halong Bay. Travels by boat to Cat Ba Island.
June 2	Returns to Hanoi and hires a motorcycle to travel southward along Highway 1.
June 7	En route stops in Hue, Hoi An, Nha Trang, and Dalat; visits the DMZ and the Ho Chi Minh trail.
June 20	Arrives in Saigon.
June 23	Hires a boat north along the Mekong River, *en route* to Cambodia. Overnights in Moc Bai. Hires a ferry to Phnom Penh.

June 24	Arrives in Phnom Penh.
June 27	Hires a boat to continue up the Mekong to Siem Reap; spends three days exploring the Angkor Wat temple complex.
June 30	Leaves Siem Reap. Flies to Vientiane, the capital of Laos.
July 1	Leaves Vientiane for Luang Prabang via Highway 13 – the only surfaced road in Laos.
July 2	Spends a week in Luang Prabang writing, teaching, and visiting Buddhist temples.
July 9	Returns to Vientiane.
July 10	Boards night train to Bangkok from Nong Khai at the Thai border.
July 11	Arrives in Bangkok.
July 17	Departs Bangkok for India.
July 18	Arrives in Calcutta.
July 20	Departs Calcutta for Varanasi, one of the most ancient living cities in India. Visits Sarnath, the site of Buddha's first sermon.
July 24	Varanasi to Khajuraho, Madhya Pradesh by bus, train, and on foot. Spends several days visiting the temples of Khajuraho.
July 27	Departs Khajuraho for Orchha by bus. Visits Jehangir Mahal and the Laxminarayana Temple.
July 28	Falls ill.
August 1	Recovers, heads north towards Agra. Visits the Taj Mahal and Agra Fort.
August 3	From Agra, moves westward towards Rajasthan and the pink city of Jaipur. Visits Sawai Jai Sing and the Amber Fort. Spends a week writing in the Hotel Diggi Palace, former home of Thakur Sahib Pratap Singh.

August 10   Returns to Delhi. Visits Jantar Mantar, the Red Fort, Connaught Place.

August 14   Boards overnight train to Calcutta. Visits Lake Gardens, home of P. Lal's *Writer's Workshop*.

August 17   Leaves Calcutta for Seoul, Korea.

August 19   Returns to Toronto, Canada.

Notes

1. The epigraph is taken from Washington Matthews, "The Night Chant, a Navaho Ceremony" (*Memoirs of the American Museum of Natural History* [New York, 1902]), as reprinted in *Poems For The Millennium*, edited with commentaries by Jerome Rothenberg and Pierre Joris, Los Angeles, CA: University Of California Press, 1995, pp. 45-46.

2. See: Glass, Jesse. "Lecturing on Walt Whitman and Emily Dickinson in China." *Literary Review* 39 (Summer 1996), p. 620.

3. See: Zedong, Mao "Swimming", as reprinted in *Modern Literature of the Non-Western World*, edited by Clerk, Jayana and Ruth Siegel, London: Longman, 1995, pp. 48-49.

4. Compare with: Greene, Graham. *The Lawless Roads*, London: Penguin, 1947, p 79.

5. Compare with: Roethke, Theodore. "Cuttings (Later)", *The Lost Son and Other Poems,* New York: Doubleday, 1948.

Daniel Sendecki was born in 1975 in Montreal, Canada. He studied at the University of Waterloo (B.A., 1998) before receiving his Master's Degree in English Language and Literature from Queen's University in Kingston, Ontario. In 2002 he taught at the Language Education Centre at Chonnam National University, Gwangju, South Korea. *Strange Currencies is* his first book.

OTHER TITLES FROM AHADADA

Ahadada Books publishes poetry. Preserving the best of the small press tradition, we produce finely designed and crafted books in limited editions.

SONG TO AREPO

Jesse Glass, ISBN: 3-89810-184-3

"His rhythms are vigorous, his imagery is strong and inventive; and his language has, in places, a burly force that reminds me of Geoffrey Hill."
—Jane Somerville, *The American Book Review*

THE BOOK OF DOLL

Jesse Glass, ISBN: 3-89810-185-1

"The images and figures of Glass's poetry are usually not of the physical world, but rather metaphysical or psychological manifestations of deep-seated fears, desires and aspirations. Glass's approach to human problems and situations is indirect and elusive. He asks questions without expecting answers and he often seems to be stepping aside as the fantastic creatures he creates charge at him, perhaps suggesting a sly humor."
—Karl Young, *The Shepherd Express*

MAKE DEATH DIE

Jesse Glass, ISBN: 3-89810-186-X

". . . poems of an almost claustrophobic intensity."
—Polly Bird, *New Hope International Review*

AGAINST THE AGONY OF MATTER

Jesse Glass, ISBN: 3-89810-187-8

"Glass has a great gift for images."
—L. Kiew, *New Hope International Review*

For these and other titles from Ahadada, visit
www.ahadadabooks.com